Contents

T0351323

Written by
Alison Hawes
Illustrated by
Stephen Elford

Series editor **Dee Reid**

P Pearson

Characters

Luka

Anna

Tom

Sophie

Miss Smith

The Head

Tricky words

- childish
- angrily
- whispered
- groaned
- soaked
- worse
- excluded
- super-glued

Read these words to the student. Help them with these words when they appear in the text

Introduction

Luka was a joker but everyone at Aspen Road School was fed up with his jokes. Anna was angry with him but Tom told her to play a joke on Luka. One day Luka set off the fire alarm to get out of a maths test but everyone got soaked in the rain. Then someone played a joke on Luka.

Joker

Luka was a joker.
But everyone at Aspen Road School was fed up with his jokes.
Some of Luka's jokes were very childish - like the day he put a toy spider on Miss Smith's desk - and some of his jokes were not very funny at all.

One day, Luka put Anna's lunch in the bin and put a stone in her lunch box.

"Oh, grow up, Luka!" she said angrily. "That's not funny."

Tom let Anna share his lunch.

"Don't get angry at Luka," he whispered. "Get back at him!"

"You mean I should play a joke on Luka?" said Anna.

"Why not?" said Tom. "He plays jokes on us."

"OK," Anna grinned. "Leave it to me!"

After lunch, Sophie saw Luka on the way to maths. "We've got that maths test today," she groaned. "There won't be time for a test today," grinned Luka.

"What do you mean, there won't be time?" Sophie asked.
Luka laughed. "Just wait and see!"
"What are you up to, Luka?" she said.
But Luka had gone.

As Sophie went into maths, the fire alarm went off.
Everyone groaned and went outside.
It was raining.

Luka caught up with Sophie outside.
"Did you do that?" she whispered. "Did you set off the fire alarm?"
Luka just laughed.
"But Luka that's not funny," said Sophie.
"We're all soaked!"

Two fire engines raced up Aspen Road and into the school grounds.
Miss Smith rushed up to the Head.

"I think Miss Smith saw you set off the alarm," said Sophie. "She keeps looking our way and pointing at you."
Luka went pale.

The Head went to speak to the firemen.
The firemen were very angry.

"I think you're in trouble!" said Sophie.
Luka looked at the ground.

Soon everyone knew it was Luka who had set off the fire alarm.
Everyone was very angry with him.
They had got soaked for nothing.
Sophie and Luka went back to maths.

"There isn't time for the maths test," said Miss Smith. "So, you will miss your break to make up the time." Everyone was even more angry with Luka after that!

But things got even worse for Luka after maths.
Miss Smith took him to see the Head.
"Playing with the fire alarm isn't a joke,"
said the Head.

The Head gave Luka a letter.
It said he was excluded from
school for two days.
Then he sent Luka home.

Luka went to get his bike.
He tried to undo his bike lock.
But the lock was jammed.
He couldn't understand it.

"What's up?" asked Anna on her way to music.
"Some joker has super-glued my bike lock!" he said angrily.
"That's not funny!" grinned Anna.

Quiz //////////////////////

Text comprehension

Literal comprehension
p4 What joke did Luka play on Anna?
p13 Why were the class very angry with Luka?

Inferential comprehension
p10 Why does Luka go pale?
p16 Who super-glued Luka's bike lock?
p16 Why does Anna say 'That's not funny?'

Personal response
- How would you feel if you were excluded from school?
- Have you ever played a trick on someone?

Word knowledge

p4 Why is there an apostrophe after 'Anna'?
p4 Find an adverb.
p5 Find 5 types of punctuation.

Spelling challenge

Read these words:

won't   caught   under

Now try to spell them!

Ha! Ha! Ha!

What do cows use to do their sums?

A Cow-culator!

Find out about

- all the April Fools' jokes that happen on 1st April.

Tricky words

- newspapers
- reported
- silent
- company
- recharging
- feature
- viewers
- similar

Read these words to the student. Help them with these words when they appear in the text.

Introduction

1st April is April Fools' Day. There are always April Fools' jokes in the newspapers, on TV and on the internet. On one April Fools' Day, the BBC reported that chips were to be banned from all schools. On another April Fools' Day, Walkers said they had made the world's first silent crisps. Would you have fallen for any of these jokes?

APRIL

1

April Fool!

1st April is April Fools' Day.
There are always April Fools' jokes in the
newspapers, on TV and on the internet.
Here are some of the jokes that have
been played.
Would you have fallen for any of them?

No chips!

On Ist April 2003, the BBC reported
some very bad news for all school children.
Chips were to be banned from all schools!
Luckily for you, it was just an April Fools' joke!

Silent crisps

On 1st April 2009, a newspaper said Walkers crisps had made the world's first **silent** crisps!
You had to eat them with a spoon.

Gum charger

Also on 1st April 2009, a company called ReBubble said it had made a charger for recharging your chewing gum. You just had to plug in the charger and leave your gum in it for a few hours and it would be as good as new!

Children fly for free

On 1st April 2004, the Ryanair website joked
that children could fly for free on their planes…
for as long as they could hang on!

LivePoke

On 1st April 2007, Facebook said
they had a new feature.
Instead of sending a poke icon
to your friends, Facebook would
send a real person round to your
friends to poke them!

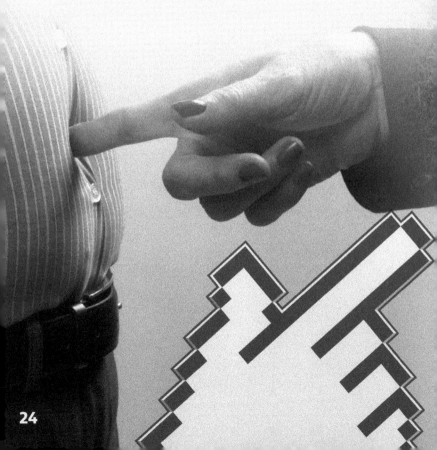

Upside down YouTube

On 1st April 2009, YouTube played a trick by
playing some of their videos upside down!
They said viewers should turn upside down
to see them better!

Left-handed mobile

The day **before** April Fools' Day in 2004, it was reported that Virgin Mobile had made the world's first mobile for left-handed people.

The joke was a day early but it was still an April Fools' joke!

Left-handed burger

A similar trick was played in America
on 1st April 1998.
Burger King said they had made
the world's first left-handed burger.
Some people fell for the joke and
even tried to buy left-handed burgers!

Nessie found

On 1st April 1972, the newspapers said that
the body of Nessie, the Loch Ness Monster,
had been found.
Reporters from all over the world came to
Loch Ness to write about the monster,
but it was just an April Fools' joke!

Tartan sheep

On 1st April 2009, a newspaper
printed a photo of some tartan sheep.
The newspaper said the tartan sheep had
been bred by a Scottish farmer.
But he had just painted them!

Most April Fools' jokes are just good fun.
But some April Fools' jokes can go very wrong!
On 1st April 2003, a shop worker in America
called her boss. She said the shop was being
robbed by armed men!

The boss didn't know it was just a joke.
He called the police and the
shop worker was fired!

Quiz ///////////////////

Text comprehension

Literal comprehension

p21 What April Fools' joke did Walkers crisps play?

p23 What was the joke in the Ryanair offer?

Inferential comprehension

p27 Why might people believe that there were left-handed burgers?

p29 How can you tell some people go to a lot of trouble to make an April Fools' joke?

p31 How can April Fools' jokes go wrong?

Personal response

- Have you ever fallen for an April Fools' joke?
- Have you ever tricked someone on April Fools' Day?

Word knowledge

p23 Find a word that means 'for no charge'.

p23 Why are there dots after the word 'planes'?

p31 What two words are combined to make the word 'didn't'?

Spelling challenge

Read these words:

school   their   after

Now try to spell them!

Ha! Ha! Ha!

Where did the sheep go to get his haircut?

To the baa-baa shop!